WORDS OF A FEATHER HAWKED TOGETHER

WORDS OF A FEATHER HAWKED TOGETHER

LINDA MARIE HILTON

atmosphere press

Published by Atmosphere Press

Cover design by Josep Lledó

atmospherepress.com

Dedication

This volume of poetry is dedicated to

both of my grandmothers,

each of whom,

in the depths of the Great Depression,

had the guts to

elope with a man of a different faith.

Table of Contents

Definition

Poetry is an
ancient vase filled with
contemporary blossoms.

Why Form?

Earth is a form, turning regularly;
Orbiting the sun which whizzes through space;
Formed of atoms, formed into molecules:
Everywhere we look, nature is as orderly as a book.
Regularity rules the day especially in the flowering
We await in the month of May.
Identical wheat berries we seek to grind to fine exact flour
With which identical loaves to make.
We pray our children perfectly formed will be
In rhymes we delight as though they were the light;
Light bulbs each needlessly (?) perfectly formed.
Does function follow form?
Or does form follow function?
The earth's tilt causes seasons
But is that the function?
Does the human form exist to dominate the planet?
Or as a biogeneticist's "Let's see if bipedalism works."
We know our form but not our function:
Will we ever even at unction?
Who will memorize your poetry
For all time if it does not rhyme?
(rhyme: a matching form our mouths make).
Does Trekies' Q have a shape?
In Childhood's End do we escape
From form as all chemists and physicists know?

Or energize to a form beyond our comprehension?

We live in cosets, do you hear me Kosiak?

Elements and Other Poems Inspired by Nature

The Five Elements
Earth, Air, Fire, Water, and Metal

Earth

Blue and green spheroid viewed from on high,
Revolving atilt in our sol's sky,
We gnomes call her Gaia, earth, or just plain home,
It's not the sort of place anyone can buy.
Its lushest places are yards deep in loam,
Covered in grasses o'er which herbivores roam,
Dotted with copses, mottes, of trees galore
In which initiates meet to read rites from tomes.
We call this the ground, parts of which are moors:
Wild strange places where the rain often pours.
For the ground, land , dirt, is covered with a plantacious shirt:
An abundance of flora and fauna would one see on a ground
tour.
Ash Wednesdays words do not render us hurt:
"from dirt we come and we will return unto dirt".

Wind

Invisible partner of dancing trees,
Rustling ruffling thief of leaves.
Provider of thermals for soaring birds
Conveyer of aromas of fragrant teas,
Bringer of nimbuses in a herd,
So those outsides their loins will gird
In advance of plummeting drops of rain
In a drenching shower is the only word.
Else will the wind carry down our lanes
With clouds of dust to pummel the vanes
Atop our home which point or twirl
In each moment of the wind's reign.
Winds which cause our flags to unfurl
And cause all leaves to constantly birle.

Volcano

Smoking, steaming, spewing ash,
Around its crater ne'er be rash.
Knowing what lurks inside the cauldron
Down its slopes be prepared to dash.
Noxious vapors make a rash head a bald one
Even if the volcano's in its doldrums.
Lava flows and stays hot a long time
If you're near them be prepared to run.
Carefully plan your bird watching climb,
You must be able to turn on a dime.
"The earth's representative of fire you be,
Of the elements, one that's prime".
Volcanoes rising from the sea
Creating new worlds for God to see.

Rain Sonnet

Rain, rain, now and again
Upon mossy banks where
Previously I have lain
Saturates the air
As it soaks the tree bark
Never missing its mark
From morn until dark.
My sun bleached sarks
No longer fly in the breeze
But drip, drip from the line
Each long lace trimmed sleeve
Twisted like a bine.
Rain, rain, fall everyplace
Especially on sleeves edged with lace.

Metal

The glinting scintillating sound
Of a sword drawn, no longer bound,
Shining captivating, steeling,
Momentarily it will pound
Metal to test another's mettle.
Striking swift with a sore to settle
Scything, swirling, striking,
Rending the air about an opponent
A metaphorical thicket of nettles.
Fluid tidal motions by ductile electrons
Cut the air while rapidly running current along.
Crystal form lends a malleable bent,
Sinuous shapes are now long gone,
Murderous rage has been given vent,
Now kiss your queen for whom you were meant.

Other Poems Inspired by Nature

Untitled

Fog like batting pulled over my eyes:
I must remember each shaped bush on the twisted path
Amongst the hills to find my way home.

Time

The tidal bore is filled once more
With flotsam, jetsam, and fish galore.
It's high time this morn's high tide brought
The sea's bounty to my front door.
Yesterdays spent fishing for naught
Have left my nets and hopes tied up in knots,
Again aground on life's neap tide,
Each catch to my chest have I claucht.
Seaweed and dolphins catch a ride!
The phenomenon is world wide,
Netting for our table a gold mine.
The ocean 's strength let none deride:
Today a feast tomorrow a famine,
Or a winter without an ermine.

Lentils

Small round seed, red or green,
Much more nutritious than any bean.
So when it's a night to serve legumes
Cook lovely lentils and don't be mean.
Don't serve stuff you picked in a coomb
On the wicked way to the edge of doom,
Serve lentils full of folic acid so
To ward away your need for a tomb
By stimulating new cell growth
Not just hair or nails but both
Combine lentils with brown rice
And all seven proteins: an oath!
You'll be as full as cheese fed mice
And defer being a corpse as cold as ice.

Red Eye

Night wends its way, a dark asphalt ribbon
Embedded with ground glass like the stars in the sky
Wending its way westward, always away from the dawn
Trying to stay in the dark, trying to hide from the song of the lark
Staying the dew on the lawn, resting on the tongue of death's mawn
Which sticks further and further west
Never quite catching up with tomorrow, trying to stay in yesterday.
West coast beaches reached, land is breached.
Riding out on the ebbing tide, but the tide turns, waiting for no man;
Forcing night the other way, to confront eventually the dawing day;
Illuminating the sides of the safe dark roadway
Shoulders, wild grass, shrubs, then trees, as the tide recedes so does the sea.
But the road is not tidal now having been washed ashore over the dunes
But bound for the east coast. As the sun rises it does boast:
"Night! stop trying to fight the inevitable appearance of daylight
Do not contend or challenge my might.
In my orbit you are bound, a way out cannot be found.
For now night you are gone, until I bid you come again

And let God's creation rest, so that at dawn they'll look their best.
Night you are my other half, all God's creatures mighty distaff.
So go now night and rest yourself
In twelve hours you may leave your shelf."

On the Theme of Orbit

Hurtling, curving through deep space
Each of us in our own place
Our heavenly bodies constantly spin
At a comfy continuous regular pace.
A full circle each day : the yin
Of our worlds out from which we in
A crystal ball on the universe gaze
To view much but not escape: a win
Invisibly tethered to the Sun ablaze
Were we not planets we'd be in a daze.
Three dizzy dance motions, yet no bumper cars
Such skewed regularity does amaze.
I am voluptuous Venus, you are thewy Mars
We gaze at each other through Love's bars:
Held by the Sun in our circular track
Non ellipsoid actions our lives do lack.

How Blew a Hurricane

calling her a hurricane
is an example of caconymy
leaving all in her path
in a state called catatonic.
an economy of letters
would render her name wrath
unleashed in a cacophony
of howling wind and drenching rain
followed by rioting beyond imagine
rendering all in her path
in a state of anomie.

Life in the Semi-Arid West

Resplendent with spring blooms and leaves of grass
Vibrant colors dot the landscape en masse:
The mountain meadow beckons to us:
We world weary souls upon a mountain pass,
Hiking high dirt paths impassable to a bus,
Living lives with a minimum of fuss.
This meadow a mountain's luxurious lap.
We rest here in peace, while bilious blisters we cuss.
We soak up peaceful beauty that is not on any map,
Amidst singing swallows we drift to a dream:
Of trees not near a bubbling tap:
"We thirst!" they cry: "for water from that stream!"
We awake to discover we've dreamed as a team.
A second lunch, we stretch, and go on our way,
Until through the meadow a slender stream does gleam,
And beyond, below where the stream does not lay
Is withered grass, faded blooms not gay,
Drooping trees beg moisture with haunting looks.
Our shovels we find, we work without pay:
A shallow channel we dig, zigzagging from the brook:
Old fashioned irrigation, not in any book:
A narrow channel traversing the slope
Debauching into a grove of sered trees: a shady nook.
Back up at the stream we connect our sinuous trope,
Removing the last foot of dirt: soon a gleaming rope
Of crystal clear water surges gurgling through

And heads downhill at a fairly brisk lope.
We camp thereabouts, a night we'll not rue,
We eat heartily, one tired, happy crew.
To sleep under sweet breezes, resting 'til morn;
Deeply dreaming til dawn comes due,
Greeting us with a sight no longer sered and worn:
But green grasses and bright blooms: acres of flora totally
reborn.

To One of God's Creations

Where in the universe are you going,
fast outpacing a Boeing?
Galaxies swirling, their atoms dirling,
Stellar clouds birling, comets hurling.
the big bang with a twang
releasing a gang of stellar objects hang
spinning with energy, systems towards entropy;
yet organized plenary consummates synergy.
Pushing into the jaws of death
expelling death outwards with life's breath
into the vast beyond conquering,
glowing universe where are you knowingly going?

Leavings

Fall has left leaves lying
Twirling, dirling, birling to usher in
Winter's icy winds;
Fleeing pell-mell around
To this earth by gravity bound
'Til some Everest reared up high
Causes them to dwindle to a sigh.
Each leaf a matrix of summer's
Memories in chemistry encased
To lie in slumber without any haste
Ending to slowly release organic compounds
Read as the past year's coffee grounds.
Each day a molecule now to lie
All events recorded in tiny dies,
Taken up again by whatever plant
Memories as such will forever rant.
Flora as such all history know
Preserved as in glacier's layers of snow
Therefore all trees be superlatively wise
Composed of germ's memories as molecule's eyes.

Oatmeal

Please don't be so cruel, do not call me gruel.
Milk, honey, and apricots make me an entire meal.
A crop for cool weather alongside the heather,
A hearty addition to scones so we will not be bare bones,
Full of iron and potassium I contain the doctor's dictum,
For strength of your heart and legs like a hart
I yield stamina galore, with cinnamon I do not bore.
I strengthen your body's core and keep open health's door.
I give your day a good start and ensure you'll do your part
To keep pace with life's drum and on a harp gaily strum.
I fend off illness' moans so you may work to pay loans.
You'll look good in tooled leather, your pack'll be light as a feather
On the market is no better deal, please, please call me oatmeal,
please don't be so cruel, do not call me gruel.

Tree Sonnet

Soaring arcs of carbon chains
Reaching upwards towards the sky
I fear they will fall I know not why,
Or how gravity they may defy.
Coaxing from clouds streams of pouring rain
Doing that over and over again
To heavy by shape balancing tensile flexible strength
'Gainst gravity gaily grandiosely gallivanting
In the winds that wrap the world.
Gone entish now fixed in the ground
With branches that mimic roots
Each kind of tree a different shaped leaf
Myriads of which form living wreaths
Beauty that beguiles, magic is afoot.

Blue Hurricane

A category Four is at the door
but not for long, it'll be never more.
a dark grey bluish black towering cloud
with raging gale winds ahowling aloud.
when it made landfall it hit earth so hard
it blew the seawall as if it were a card.
over land it quickly becomes so weak
evaporating water it does seek
with which to replenish dense falling rain
so it may tumble earthward once again.
as it weakens it begins mumbling
"Category three is very humbling".
it lessens more and becomes so forlorn,
Category two just cannot be borne.
it slowly begins to sing the blues
its whirling system starting to slue.
soon its winds rip the reigning clouds apart
so merry birds again may swoop and dart.
the blue black storm may now bluishly weep
as from the sky the wind merrily sweeps
the blue hurricane's last remaining sigh,
replacing the blue storm with an azure sky.

A Walled Garden in Fall

Underneath the rhododendrons
Pine needles have softly fallen
A cushion redolent of sap
Oozing out of a pine's bark's gaps.
Underneath the rhododendrons
Under oaks dropping their acorns
Squirrels scamper cheerfully about
Acorns galore making them stout.
Underneath the rhododendrons
Eighty thousand leaves have fallen
Awaiting my trusty red rake
Just barely ahead of snowflakes.
Underneath the rhododendrons
I lotus upon my sit-upon
Steeping myself in nature's wrap
Around the world, a pseudonap.
Underneath the rhododendrons
Earth's creatures live in a heaven.

To Barley

Unassuming little beige grain,
Not allowed as payment for a kane.
But right at home as a legume
In a soup with lamb is it fain.
Its aroma does not boom
But gently, softly fills a room.
A hearty whole grain full of boron
Leaving women content with a loom,
Sleeping well and rising at dawn,
With never, ever a face that is wan;
Making it possible to be a mom,
While looking as lovely as a swan.
Barley, boron, such a nom!
The stars of saveyouruterus.com.

Pond

Water pooled in sunshine and in shade
Mostly blue, motley grey, algal green
Ripples here, wind-blown waves over there
Splashes of frogs and swishing of the fish
Blue, grey, green, mix, meld, mélange, then part
Bulrushes sway, sweet sunny midday
Refracted light shifts, wind the limbs shifts.
Are invisible nymphs faces reflected
Or are our fantasies by nature rejected?
Instead absorb the beauty of the scene
View it as an almost awake dream
And thread to bind life's unraveled seams.

Carbon to be Copied

Gathering carbon from the air
Funneling a building block from everywhere
From hundreds of leaf bearing twigs
Coalescing into branches,
Further in to the trunk,
Plunging into the earth to
The ultimate mystery:
The truth of what makes trees grow

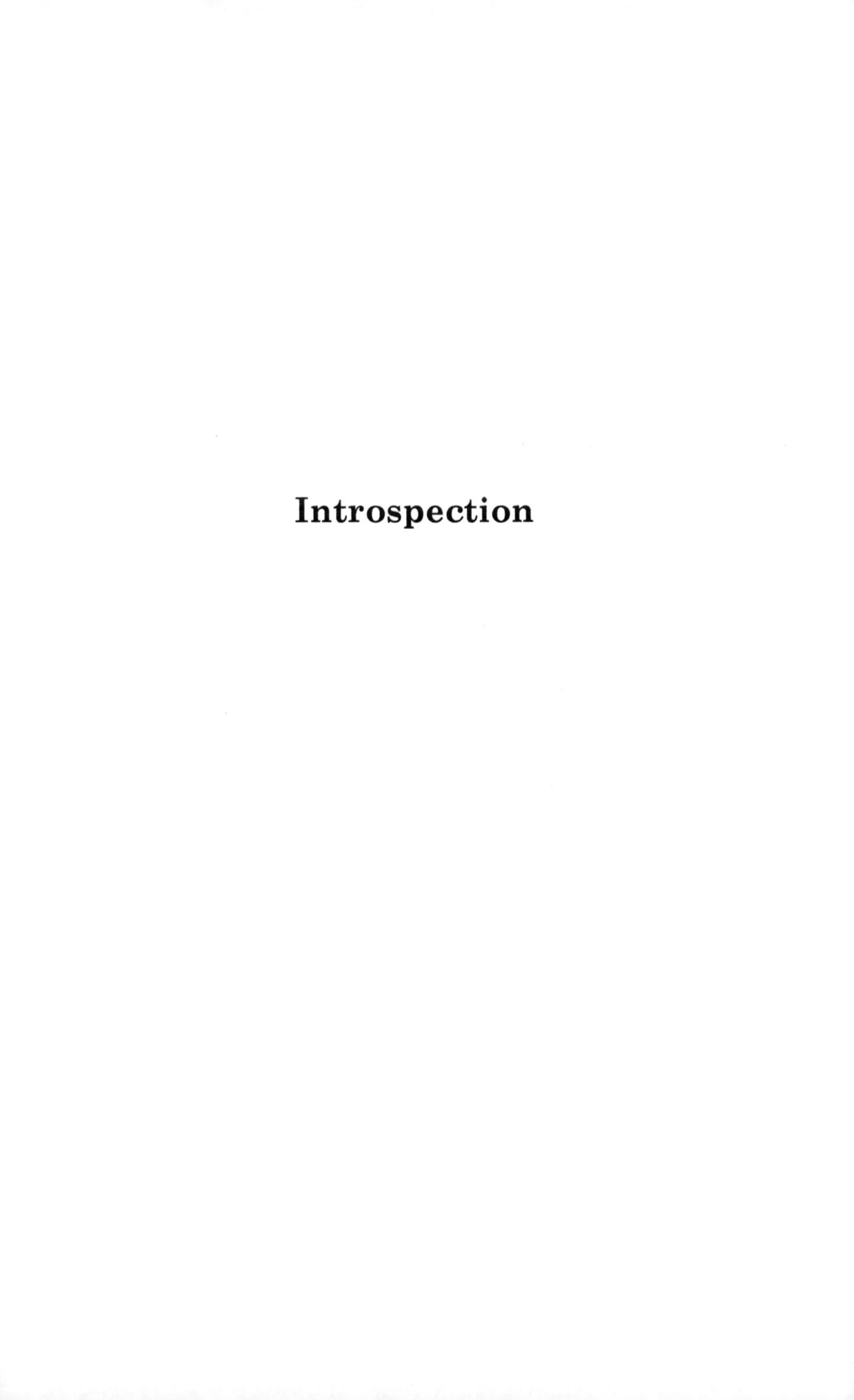

Introspection

To the Beginning

Oh! Death be not Proud, thou art not allowed.
We need not your shroud; our fields are all plowed.
We are of the earth, our hunger is dearth,
the spring will give birth from earth's belly's girth.
From breath upon dung Enkidu was sprung;
with breath from his lungs rain from clouds he wrung.
the most welcome rain brought forth fields of grain.
give thanks in the fane, our hunger will wane.
Now harvest the grapes, transport them in capes;
Plenty! our mouths gape, fine garlands we'll drape.
The wine will be ample: grape juice is purple!
Now we all trample before we can sample.
With bread and wine attain the divine.
Death is a-dying as leaves on the vine
In winter turned brown then a-falling down
like seeds early sown dead leaves can abound
In life giving plants to give death the rants.
Since Gaia us grants deer in meadows prance.
By death trampling death nirvanah neareth,
heaven appeareth, humbling You, proud Death.

Words

Words caress
With such finesse
Why use them to slam
As if you don't give a damn.
Words are subtle
Used for rebuttal.
They coax, they hoax,
They boast, they roast.
For the New Year's
They toast.
Your fancies they tickle,
Your memories they pickle,
They are exact and never fickle.
We expand our minds
With books bought for a dime.
We fancy ourselves enlightened
As we have broadened
Our horizons to include
The length and breadth of the world.
Words caress
With such finesse
Why use them to slam
As if you don't give a damn.

Lady Lie in Waiting

Lust lain in the dust
Accumulates yet more dust
Dirt, yet, flotsams and jetsam
Loess lain languishing as do all yins
(wind borne seeds)
Awaiting accumulating patience
For yang's fang of passion
Intruder in to the dust
Catalyst sparking seemingly
Life's dross into life's germ
Slowly unfolding like a humungous plant
Already made yet crammed into seed
Lady lie in waiting
If such dust as I you will trust
For I would give you a copy of yourself,
Indeed all my pelf
Lady lie in waiting
For an eventual mating
I would never love but you
I beg you say I do.

Wayfaress

Alone I wander
Over dusty roads, pack heavy,
gathering breezy sunshine
sleeping under trees
Alone with nature's way.
The un-included
Not in. not hip. Not with it.
too square, too fair, I never dare.
I don't belong, my hair's too long.
I read too much, I never touch.
Within a form I find a norm.
I sometimes rhyme in duple time,
Of any clique, I'm not within.
I'm always outside, looking in.

In the Company of Poets

I don't mind spending my time
With those of you who are not mimes.
You contemplate the word
As though it were a bird,
Seeking for each one a place
Where it will not be crushed by a mace,
But instead a niche from which to shine
As if it were a gem found in a mine.
It is not so very much work
To illustrate a word not as a bork
Instead as cutlery beside a plate
Whose place in the table design is enough to elate.
I don't mind spending my time
With those of you who refuse to rhyme.

What I Wanted To Be When I Grew Up (#2)

My dream was to be an orchestral musician,
in all the world the only proper position
from which to perform B's "the music of the spheres".
To tone, time, and timbre we correctly adhere.
emote within parameters to a divine
peace, to resonate with the universe, a wine
so heady. we cling together, tempo steady:
golden ratio, Fibonacci, we're ready;
transcending all earthly cares, the devil beware
We're gone from his clutches, vanished into thin air.
sound waves created sent far out of human sight
ringing in time, with a cesium atom's might.
playing over daily breadlike act of contrition
dedicated to music of our own volition.

To Kulka

PTSD, PTSD, why won't you let me be?
Years upon years have passed since I came back
From far across the briny sea!
From a land of no coffee but tons of tea
Drunk best when laced with jack
Cupped in one hand, a girl on the other knee.
Even though for this the MP's charge a fee
To let one while away a day in a shack
That has a door but never lock and key.
Then you claim you lay in mud alee
From artillery fire bent on being wrack
Far worse than that childhood stings of a bee.
From a day spent in a metaphorical lea
You return with your pack to a filthy track
Meandering through foxholes as far as the eye can see.
To venture out of a fox hole brings taunts of "nene",
So you'll stay under cover like a wrinkled sack
Until darkness when like romans we'll form a Vee
Piercing the enemy's front' heroes we will be!

My Pisa Workspace

Laying vapidly on my cluttered desk
Is scattered my collection of unread books:
Some poetry: Ashbery, Tennyson,
Telemann trio sonatas stacked on
Langston Hughes weighted down with Robert Frost
Enlaced with my unfinished catalogue
Summing my life's work, my invented forms,
Some luscious unique notecard designs to
Tempt florid missives from working women
On *A Year in the Life of a Poet*
Readerless at an open mic as yet
Yielding to Shakespeare and Spenser's *Faerie Queene.*

Not the Cherry Tree

For moon's months I've penned languid love poems
Without ever revealing his known name
Love birds we're nestled snug, a tree's phloem
We curl around each other somewhat tame,
Are nurtured 'til our love became august:
Nothing more grand than love's soaring old oak
Shielding our secret lust lain in the dust
Duty and honor serve only to stoke
Your cameo against my camisole
Courage in and of itself the alpha
Surrounds me treelike, renders me once whole
We are the other's august omega.
Revel in our reluctance to reveal
Ennobled, bound by our secret fealty!

Self Portrait

I have told you time and again
That I am neither a thespian
Nor a lesbian
But instead a classical musician,
Trained in music's diction.
To live is not the play
But to live is to love to play
Tunes both bright as day
And as somber as darkest night
Where ne'er does any light
Try to shine bright.
To play is to live,
To play is to love, to coo as a dove
To play is to be alive.
One's playing is one's wife,
One's playing is one's life.

Whither Love?

Love you elude me
As I pursue you 'cross the earth.
Love you delude me
As I peruse the absolute dearth
Of Beauty in my life
Which is winter's discontent.
Evil's just too rife
Even the trees are all bent
In this wasteland there's no water,
No glint of hopeful metal can I find.
Love's spouse no ring brought her,
To him her to eternally bind.
You, Love, money cannot buy
Coinless waifs starved for food, for you,
Precious hoped for one priced sky high
Eludes us in the depths of a vast bayou
Where metals offered to the gods
Lie buried in silty murk,
Found not by thrusting rods
Nor by prayers in a kirk.
Love, you foot-free ethereal sprite
For you my desire always unaffordable,
For I, imprisoned in penury's might
Beg Fates free me from life so dull
So bereft of glint of hope,
A veritable caged hell.

I, Love, can only mope
About in my loveless cell.

To See or Not to See

Eyes see shapes, colors, depth, light.
Cognition sees friends, flowers, stairs.
Which sees more truly
Or are both necessary to
Truly see?

Ekphrastic Poems

The Best Way

"The best way to predict the future is to create it."
-Peter Drucker

Mandalas are two D crystals
Let them be three D by tweaking
Facets, folding like origami
Make a new substance each
Mandela unique, multicolored
Jewel glistening in the sun
Coaxing sulfur adjacent to
Iron adjacent to cobalt
Make many and see which will
Harness the energy of the sun
Own a fossil free future!

Bull Dancers

Stand your ground wee lithe one
For when this day is done
After you and your kith
Of the bull dancer's myth
Have each somersaulted
By grasping horns vaulted
Awing the raging crowd
Far more than a buffoon
Upon the raging bull
In a circle more full
At festivities end
Evading death's bill
In a death defying thrill.
When homeward they you send
We will wait well mounted
And sweep down uncounted
To sweep you all away
To live another day
You need not death defy
Instead your dreams will fly
In gentler climes you'll live
You needn't your life give
As adults to defy
This evil is our joy
Better tasks we'll give you,
Even pairs of leather shoes.

Weekly, A Set of Seven Poems For the Modern Corporate Woman

Always a Day of Hope

Monday morning, no more snoring,
Are we rested, or even interested?
New leaf day so forget last week's fray.
Warmer, cooler, weather wardrobe changer.
Construction, obstruction, commuters' moot objections.
Same job, new job, management's change ups.
Old paper, new forms, loose shamrock corms:
Demand a new pot but you lost your parking spot.
By noon are you weary or close to just plain teary.
But at least last week must now be meek
As fresh clients do you seek with which to speak.
Monday always starts anew like a fresh pot of coffee put on to brew.
The entire week still a blank slate, maybe there'll even be time for a date.

Tuesday

Terrible Tuesday has already arrived,
Monday's migraine no longer contrived,
Sunday's hangover has ceased to cover
Surreptitious visits to one's lover.
No more excuses like "I'm going for juices"
Can put off that which actually produces
What was it I was hired to do?
Certainly not afternoons at the zoo.
Afternoons not written by the Moody Blues,
Tuesdays must produce two days' worth of dues.
Lazy workers should not tempt fate:
For Wednesdays deadlines never be late.
The pile in the in basket has to go down
Else look for a job out of town.

Wednesday

Witchy Wednesday lies in wait
For the usual deadlines deadly date.
The week's work best be ready
Else you'll be stuck in the eddy
Of unemployment and unemployable
No matter how eminently capable.
You'd best be ready for Wednesday's hump
Else your personal stuff will go to the dump.
Personnel insists you will be culpable
If PowerPoint presentations are purple.
Just because your success is heady
Don't go out and buy a teddy.
Learn to negotiate an appropriate pay raise
Else your reward will be some delectable cate.

Thursday

Thursday breathes a sigh of relief
Having ridden o'er Wednesday's reef.
Tonight we have church choir practice
So at work we will leave all our malice.
This week's work is a brand new leaf
Let's get to it so we may eat beef.
The weekend will be our oasis
From business decisions' accounting basis.
The boss regards the office as his fief,
About his astuteness let us not be naïf.
Not one of our errors does he miss
Nor does he intend any of us to kiss.
Therefore let us not spend this day in a kief
Or the bosses will think our jobs are not lief.

Friday

The puzzle's too hard, my cubemate thinks he's a bard,
I've made piecrust with lard and maxed out my credit card.
The weekend might not be a trip to the sea
But overtime 'til three means I'll miss high tea.
Day two of this week's workload
Requires book bound in leather dyed with woad
Containing background research in a certain mode
So I may weave this info into a node.
For a command of information yields a meticulous
presentation
Sending my mind into action amid a fraction
Of available datum to prove a contention
Thereby holding my audience's attention
By the mere mention of the breadth of the spectrum
Of data compiled into a table with nary an erratum.

Saturday

Saturday, latter day, the nothing matters day.
For once on one, not anyone, has an iota to say
About how I must always look mim,
An exercise so I don't get fatter day, to weigh
In at the gym in my plan to stay trim,
By burning calories with vim while singing hymns
Devoted to a healthy lifestyle which outlaws piles,
And runs on a calculated diet and not on a whim.
So on Saturday I plan always to go a mile
Even though other gym patrons this tends to rile
On at least eight different exercise machines
For which is required quite a bit of guile.
Saturday, Saturday, mad as a hatter day
On Saturday I may indulge in being fey.

Sunday

On the seventh day our creator rested
Knowing his creation could not be bested.
Shores cooled with gentle breezes,
On the edges of the seven seas,
Varieties of flora, fauna, fish, and fowl galore
What creature could want for more.
Mountains rearing towards the heavens
Like mighty bread made with leavens,
Skies with clouds that lour
Which pour forth water we may store,
Valleys strewn with fertile lees
Including gardens, pastures, fields of peas,
An idyllic valley where Adam and Eve were tested,
God's pension in this planet is fully vested.

En Route to Prairie

Convoluted conundrum of an old oil drum route
We wish to head NE. why are we always pointed south?
Dry dusty dirt wash boarded
Writhing way into the mountains,
Heart wrenching pauses poised
Above the curved canyon carved in the rippled rock
Of the Rocky Mountain Upthrust.
A mostly forgotten rusty road forged by
Shoshone feet now worn by a handful of
Farming families inundated by
Crazy kayakers craving cataracts of
Killer conduits of warring waters whirling.
Whipping against stony sentinels bouncing
Bounding breaking bounds until bursting
Beyond the canyon to the floodplain further south.
Travelers toiling to traverse the easy way
Past Danskin Mountain to a sweet plateau
Of cricks and grasses with a silence save for nature's sounds,
A refuge far from the maddening crowd of urban life.

Lighthouse

Soaring warning
Red and white stripes
Beacon of light
A most welcome sight
Above the sea a'roaring
Beyond the waves a'crashing
Warning of reefs known for smashing
Hapless vessels to smithereens
And of rocks known for grinding
Sailors to bone meal.
Bastion of solitude against the wind
For the keeper with his books
Spending days giving the sea piercing looks.
Signpost on a map
"only this much further to a harbor"
Outpost of where man's control
Lapses to the enormity of the sea.

To Standing Stones

Your enclosed calm, an oasis in an urban storm
showed to me by one who roller skated there
that she might study better;
transported by a modern sculptor
found in ruins after wars;
that you stones might rise again
and like the earth give shelter
to meditative thoughts
upon what is man's nature
that we might achieve gnosis.
repository of knowledge,
what might ye grey stones know?
Stand forever ye arches,
perhaps prevent war's marches.
take us in and surround us,
in physical space bound us
physically that our minds might soar,
you that are George Grey's Stones.

Facets of Mandalas

Analyze the ice
The patterns of facets are a spice
Heady and drawing one in
Fascinating spirals begin
Leading to a labyrinth
Esoteric and endless
Unfolding boldness of expression
Crystals building in succession
Distill it all to a mandala
And paint it on a wall
To see just who it enthralls
Not chance as in thrown dice
But an answer to "what is life?"

A Year in the Life of a Poet

i. January's Sonnet
ii. February
iii. Brittle Sun
iv. March Sonnet
v. Spring
vi. Rain Sonnet
vii. April Sonnet
viii. Spring
ix. Flower Power
x. To (Two) irises
xi. Peony
xii. Lilacs
xiii. To May
xiv. May Sonnet
xv. June
xvi. Roses
xvii. July
xviii. August
xix. Nooning
xx. September Dawn
xxi. September
xxii. October
xxiii. Leaf Sonnet
xxiv. Foliage Sonnet
xxv. All Hallow's Een
xxvi. Boise: On the View North of the River
xxvii. All Soul's Day
xxviii. November
xxix. December
xxx. Snow Dance
xxxi. The New Year

January's Sonnet

The dry bitter cold finds a way to creep
Into every room while we sleep,
Turning our breath into frost on windows
While o'er our sleeping heads sheep leap.
All we furless creatures the cold mows
To lie flat under heaps of skins of does,
While through leafless trees unimpeded the wind whistles
As the mercury dips towards one of winter's lows.
Insuring the fields are bereft of purple thistles
Which the wind tore off and used as missiles
To cleave eddies of swirling snow in the subzero frigid air
And dumped unceremoniously on the floor of our xysti.
Oh! to spend the month of January as a bear
In a snug den where to enter none will dare.

February

February is the cruelest month because
Its sun shines brighter than it ever was
In the crispest, driest, coldest air
Forcing us many layers of wool to wear,
In the coldest, bluest, clearest sky
So cold without wool we would surely die.
The brightness of its sun is a cruel tease
To tempt us from our warm winter's nest of ease
The blueness of the heavens bids us cry:
Oh why oh why should we stay inside?
So all bundled up out we go on a dare
Even though the weather's not fit for a bear.
A mere half hour walk coasts us with a fuzz
Of hoarfrost so thick it stiffens us with a buzz.

Brittle Sun

Dedicated to Kaden

Snow falls
Sunlight not hot enough to burn
Melts frozen footprints;
Tripping hikers;
Mud squishes under February's brittle sun.

March Sonnet

March this year you have started
Not as a lion but as a lamb:
Clear blue sky, a gentle breeze,
My shamrock is blooming.
Up have come my irises leaves.
A seat in the sun is warming
'Til it is time for the gloaming.
But yet tonight it will freeze.
This has set my heart a roaming
As a loveless winter's need
For someone to recite to me iambs
And leave me with breathless lips parted.
Perhaps this spring will to me bring
A love to make my heart sing.

Spring

Thawed frost heaved earth pierced
By green shoots enclosing buds
Damp from rain under
A warming sun swayed by a
Bird song laden gentle breeze.

Rain Sonnet

Rain, rain, now and again
Upon mossy banks where
Previously I have lain
Saturates the air
As it soaks the tree bark
Never missing its mark
From morn into the dark.
My sun bleached sarks
No longer fly in the breeze
But drip, drip from the line
Each long lace trimmed sleeve
Twisted like a bine.
Rain, rain, fall everyplace
Especially on sleeves edged with lace.

April Sonnet

April thou art so cruel this year
By now we should snowfall cease to fear.
But today a veritable blizzard fell
As though to sound cherry blooms death knell.
A storm is the job of the first of March
So that throats of thirsty shoots will not parch.
You have flooded us with blasts of cold
So that instead of young we feel old.
Now all the buds up on the larch
Fear being born through springs' dolmen arch.
In march winter and spring may yet mell
But in April we fall under Demeter's spell.
While we do not yet want rays of sun to sear
Yet we do wish to shed our coats of deer.

Spring

Sunshine on lentic
Pools of spring rain recently
Fallen from the sky
In which birds bathe and deer drink
Upon which petals float.

Flower Power

A single jonquil
Purloined from a neighbor's garden
Perfumes my rooms.

To (Two) Irises

Blooms most gorgeous, delicate, and serene
Yet yours are the shortest lived.

Peony

Multitude of petals
More than a rose
As fragrant as an entire garden
So heavy your branch droops
More than one hand can hold.

Lilacs

The aroma of pink, white, and purple blooms
Permeates the air everywhere
These fine May days
Until a rogue storm dumped inches of rain
In a day, washing the perfume and petals
Into the river,
When they should have lasted another ten
Blissful days.

To May

Oh it's spring, so let us sing
"Now is the greening of the ling"!
The sun is ours for half the day,
From the south have birds taken wing.
The sun's warm rays have softened clay
From riverbanks up yonder way
So we will dig it to make new pots
Which we'll paint in colors gay.
On the porch we'll place our cots
And untie our hair from its topknots.
The lightening of the sky at sunrise
Will awaken us before our crying tots
We'll wipe the sleep from our bright eyes
A full day of glee will we devise.

May Sonnet

May day, oh I am so gay
Winter's cold has gone far away!
Flowers are here by scores and scores
Products of many a rainy day.
Into the lake water will go my oars
Across the lake will this boat soar
The earth now wears a brand new coat
Time to delve into nature's lores.
On newly sprung willow twigs will I doat
Gathering them to weave a lovely tote
In which to carry my herbs and blooms
While singing tunes with many a high note:
A lovely day on the isle of the moon
Which will be over all too soon.

June

The blooms of June cannot come too soon,
Neither the lustrous light of June's full moon
Nor the blazing sun in a clear sky's day
Can illuminate that which is summer's boon:
A world of fragrances contained in a nosegay
Much more potent than that of fresh cut hay:
Velvet petals' divine attars reign
As costumes for all creatures fey.
Sunny days alternate with those of rain
All flora can claim to be perfectly fain
With perfect growing conditions in lovely soil
Another year's growth is to be gained.
A medley of greens and blooms in vivid colors based in oil
Against winter's whites is a magnificent foil.

Roses

Perfumed beauties of 32 petals,
A heady attar better than Ketal,
Thorny stems for protection from
Impassioned pluckers in fine fettles
Carrying guitars they occasionally strum
While perched on roofs leaning against lums.
Bunches of roses a beauty to woo
More persuasive than a bottle of rum.
Velvety petals akin to a dove's coo,
A vase of roses is the best of views.
So bring a dozen roses to the girl you love
Since most feet won't fit a glass shoe.
Then she'll fit her hands in yours like a glove
And into your ear she'll coo like a dove.

July

Now that it's July my eyes do not espy
Clouds 'cept dark nimbuses which do fly
Laden with rain threatening lightening to make
Swiftly in a vast school across the heat laden sky.
In the hot sun sun-lovers may lie and bake
As though they were a sort of delectable cake,
Alternating with quick dips meant for swimming
In the cooling waters of a mountain lake
After an early morning laziness of fishing
For the fish bite then no matter what we're wishing.
Enjoy while it lasts this awesome summer heat
And joyous long days spent in exercise which is slimming.
Spend time going places at which friends to meet
And with a smile each day early do well greet.

August

August brings on waning days
And humid heat in which to cut hay,
Ribbons to win at the state fair,
The end of days in which kids can play,
Diving into swimming holes on a dare,
Picking berries in advance of a bear,
Resigned to approaching days of school,
The yearly ritual of cutting of hair.
Back to learning the golden rule
So that none will be a fool,
(School is shade from wicked heat)
So as to learn the mind is a tool;
Used wisely and well so one can eat
Not only wheat but also meat.

Nooning

How long may you weary scythers lie
Your exhausted faced turned to the sky
Upon an unfinished stack of hay
Its fresh cut aroma bright as day
Your modest lunch already bolted
To stave the rumbling of your stomach
While blistered feet breathe free of shoes
And a wearied body refuses to move.
You lie like skins of molted snakes
Wishing lunch to be an eternal break.
You began at dawn and worked six hours
For your yearly allocation of flour.
Now you grasp at a little sleep
So a drover's whip won't make you weep,
So pray the lord your soul to keep.

September Dawn

The full moon hangs brightly
While wispy pink cirrus clouds
Announce sunrise.

September

The sun in a blue sky warm enough,
The heat of august has been sloughed.
The wheat is ripening in the field,
Bushels and bushels of grain will it yield.
Occasional warm rains keep down the dust,
Watering the garden is still a must.
Collecting from flowers gone to seed
Already fulfills next springs' need.
For a new array of bounteous blooms,
Needed to dispel all thoughts of gloom.
Across the land the gathering in
Binds once more all manner of kin.
The bounteousness of the fall harvest
Yields groaning tables for Oktoberfest.

October

The crisp cool air creates brilliant flame colored foliage
And all too soon will freeze the borage.
Foliage which eventually drifts into piles through
which we scuffle in plaid skirts, knitted wool
sweaters and berets or printed corduroy
and matching elf boots in which we look so cute
With piles of schoolbooks on our hips
Giggles issuing from our lips
Glad to be back in school
While sitting chairs made in Buhl.
Always following the golden rule
Never to swim alone in the pool
Leaves will be mulched and never burned
As we end the month with jack-o-lanterns.

Leaf Sonnet

Susurrus, susurrus, susurrus:
The leaves are whispering hush, hush
Or dancing down the street
On a vacation, on their way to meet
From photosynthesis to work-booted feet.
Rubbing softly against windows
So babies and cats will sleep,
Dancing on the ends of branches
So birds will cease to peep,
In answer to the wind's beat.
They become ornaments on benches
To be swept away by wenches
The leaves are whispering hush, hush:
Susurrus, susurrus, susurrus.

Foliage Sonnet

Red, orange, yellow are colors not mellow
But those found as a result of bellows
Being pumped by poor young fellows
To fuel a blacksmith's forge
Whose fire endless logs does gorge
In imitation of Thor's anvil in Norge
Aggregate foliage does this imitate
Each year starting with a fresh green slate
Ending in flame by Halloween's date
Red maples, orange oaks, yellow else
In a pointillistic palette which mells
These warm colors all throughout New England's dells.
Imitating fire which evade they must
In order to return once more to leaf mould dust.

All Hallow's E'en

The harvest is in with help of kin,
Leaves are falling, each one in a spin,
The pantry is full of produce in jars,
Soon we'll spend evenings in long games of gin.
There'll be time to study the stars,
And placate the neglected lars
Each morn brings a crispness to the air
And frost left on all the spars.
Tonight each man alive will take care
And to visit cemeteries not dare
For on this eve, as if with help from a djinn
Will the dead leave their coffins' lair
For a yearly night's reprieve did they win
To frighten us all from the clutches of sin.

Boise: On the View North of the River

As I walk home I see the moon rising over the foothills:
A luminous orange pumpkin hiding behind a leaf bare tree.

All Soul's Day

So on this day we kneel and pray
For soul's which are lost on their way
From their earthly graves in earthly dells
Abroad by night in search of a ray
Of hope not to burn forever in hell.
So they beseech us dip into compassion's well
Our prayers send heavenwards to bring rest
When the church summons us by bells
From an arduous ancient quest
To see if their souls have met their test
Of wrong doing for which sins must they pay
Now that they have gone into the west.
Today we beg the lord his hand to stay
From dooming souls in hell to lay.

November

November is a month of leaves
A month to pack away tank tops and bring out long sleeves
Gone are days of sunshine and ease
Now the sun is just a big tease
Giving no warmth but still shining bright
As the days slowly shorten into night
With leaves drifting down from great heights
Covering everything in sight
Scuffling through leaves leaves a wake
In which might hide cold rattlesnakes,
Causing our muscles for days to ache
After spending hours wielding a rake.
At month's end we break thanks to give
With turkey and trimmings: oh how to live!!!

December

The harvest festival has come and gone
Gone are flowers, sunshine and birds' songs.
Although the skies weep we've done no wrong
Even though this winter's sure to be long.
The first real storm has left snow on the grounds
Completely covering the shorn fields' wounds.
By our feet lay the hunting hounds:
To knitting this past springs' wool are our hands bound.
Daily the winter solstice approaches
The bitter cold on our bones encroaches.
Soon we'll hear approaching coaches
Drawn by snorting horses bringing brioches
And full of guests bringing yuletide cheer
To join us in sweetmeats and beer.

Snow Dance

Each snowflake unique
An intricate design so sleek
Perfectly symmetrical, crystalline,
It can cover anything in an icy ermine.
Fall slow, fall fast
Swirl downward in a whirling dance.
Become icing for everything is sight
Creating a panoramic delight.
By day the sunlight enhance,
By night illuminate the deer's dance.
Be the powdered sugar on hills covered in pine.
Record the skiers descent in a sinuous line
And tracks of the white rabbit so meek,
And stay forever on the world's highest peak.

The New Year

Jealous hungry Death lurks,
Its prey the dying year:
A Phoenix each year reborn
In an infinite line of Bartholomew's hats.

Allee of Trees: Haiga

Pantoum for SPLAB 2019

If you care about global warning
Plant 100 trees!
Create a squirrel highway
As far as you can see!

Each year plant 100 trees
In rows, circles, triangles
As far as y'all can see
Each kind in a kind quadrangle!

Topiary rows, circles, and triangles:
Nature's natural geometry lesson
Each kind in its kind's quadrangle
Severe storms thereby to lessen!

Each year nature's natural botany lesson
Each man plant 100 trees: bees will be aswarming
Severe storms thereby to lessen
Because you cared about global warming!

Notes

Definition: "Blue haiga" was drawn by the author using Adobe Illustrator software.

"Blue Hurricane": the prompt was for a cocktail named "Blue Hurricane," since I could find no mention of such an item on the web, I punned on the word "blue," this produced two of the poems in this section.

"Words" was written as a protest, for although I admire the skill of slam poets, it is not the only form of poetry and I personally prefer a more contemplative approach.

"My Pisa Workspace" is from the *Next Line, Please* blog; the prompt for this was to write a list poem (a poem containing a list—to list is to enumerate or to sag to one side like the Tower of Pisa) which contains at least three of the following words: listless, tory, invent, and catalogue.

The purple and pink mandala I drew using Adobe Illustrator software and was inspired by the mandala painted on a friend's round table.

"Bull Dancers" was inspired by the controversy about the bull statue on Wall Street, NYC: a woman sculptor fashioned a girl and put her in front of the bull, and this poem is my reaction to the ensuing bruhaha.

"The Road to Prairie" follows a footpath worn by Shoshone on their way to a summer camping ground and is an unpaved goat path some of which is best driven, even in an automatic, in first gear.

"Lighthouse" was inspired by memories of visiting Twin Lights lighthouses and the nearby beach on vacations to visit my father's family in Portland, Maine.

"To Standing Stones" was inspired by my memory of visiting the Cloisters Museum in NYC many years ago (I lived in NYC more than a decade).

"A Year in the Life of a Poet" is so named to evoke Solzhenitsyn's famous novel, and was inspired by the analytic process by which ancient humans analyzed the movement of celestial bodies with nothing but their eyes, and thereby created the form we call The Year. It is also a celebration of the year, the seasons, and all that is natural in the passage of Time. There are 31 poems because that is the number of syllables in a tanka.

The word "nooning" is a meal eaten at noon. This poem was inspired by Van Gogh's painting "Haystacks."

Imagery used in the last poem, "The New Year," was taken from the creation myth in the Upanishads and the Dr. Seuss book, *Bartholomew and the 500 Hats.*

Since I have been in near death experiences three times in my life, to me each year I live is more beautiful than the last. This cycle of poems was finished August 2012.

The photo of the allee was taken by me in a local park.

The pantoum was written in response to the problem of global warming and the resultant climatic change (I must note that seven billion homo sapiens give off a lot more heat than one billion homo sapiens).

Acknowledgements

The following poems were published in the *San Gabriel Valley Poetry Quarterly*:

"Wind", "Rain", and "Metal" from "Elements"; "Self Portrait (1)", "Whither Love" (In "Free Love 2".)

The following poems were written for and posted to the *Next Line, Please* poetry blog hosted by *The American Scholar* website:

"How Blew a Hurricane", "Life in the Semi Arid West", "To One of God's Creations", "Blue Hurricane", "To the Beginning", "Lady Lie in Waiting", "What I Wanted to be When I Grew Up", "My Pisa Workspace", "Not the Cherry Tree", "Bull Dancers", "To Standing Stones".

About Atmosphere Press

Atmosphere Press is an independent, full-service publisher for excellent books in all genres and for all audiences. Learn more about what we do at atmospherepress.com.

We encourage you to check out some of Atmosphere's latest releases, which are available at Amazon.com and via order from your local bookstore:

I Would Tell You a Secret, poetry by Hayden Dansky

Aegis of Waves, poetry by Elder Gideon

Footnotes for a New Universe, by Richard A. Jones

Streetscapes, poetry by Martin Jon Porter

Feast, poetry by Alexandra Antonopoulos

River, Run! poetry by Caitlin Jackson

Poems for the Asylum, poetry by Daniel J. Lutz

Licorice, poetry by Liz Bruno

Etching the Ghost, poetry by Cathleen Cohen

Spindrift, poetry by Laurence W. Thomas

A Glorious Poetic Rage, poetry by Elmo Shade

Numbered Like the Psalms, poetry by Catharine Phillips

Verses of Drought, poetry by Gregory Broadbent

Canine in the Promised Land, poetry by Philip J. Kowalski

PushBack, poetry by Richard L. Rose

Modern Constellations, poetry by Kendall Nichols

Whirl Away Girl, poetry by Tricia Johnson

About the Author

Born and raised in Massachusetts, blue-eyed Linda Marie Hilton dreamed of being an oboist in a symphony orchestra. Studying oboe in NYC a year, then running out of money, she worked as an accounting clerk, returning to night school to obtain a BSc in Accounting from CUNY. She worked several years in public accounting and in the evenings played her oboe in a community orchestra. She moved to the Pacific Northwest for her health and has lived there more than 25 years. Once again starving she became a poet. She enjoys reading, writing, gardening, hiking, knitting, designing and crocheting beaded lace, the beautiful wilderness, bicycling, and being a practical environmentalist.

www.ingramcontent.com/pod-product-compliance
Ingram Content Group UK Ltd.
Pitfield, Milton Keynes, MK11 3LW, UK
UKHW042002190726
13854UKWH00005B/2132